Carving
the
Mariachi

Ballo Rebora

Schiffer Publishing Ltd®

4880 Lower Valley Road, Atglen, Pa 19310

Other Schiffer Books by Ballo Rebora
Carving a Bull Fighter & the Bull. ISBN: 9780764329104.
$14.95.

Other Schiffer Books on Related Subjects
29 Cowboy Patterns for Carvers. Al Streetman. ISBN: 076430187X.
$12.95.
Carving a Street-Corner Band. Al Streetman. ISBN: 0764313282.
$14.95.
Carving Desperados with Tom Wolfe. Tom Wolfe. ISBN:
0764300970. $12.95.
Carving Mountain Men with Cleve Taylor. Cleve Taylor. ISBN:
0764306545. $14.95.
Carving Out the Wild West with Tom Wolfe: The Saloon. Tom
Wolfe. ISBN: 0887403689. $12.95.
Cowboy Carving with Cleve Taylor. Cleve Taylor. ISBN:
0887406416. $12.95.

Published by Schiffer Publishing Ltd.
4880 Lower Valley Road
Atglen, PA 19310
Phone: (610) 593-1777; Fax: (610) 593-2002
E-mail: Info@schifferbooks.com

For the largest selection of fine reference books on this
and related subjects, please visit our web site at **www.
schifferbooks.com**
We are always looking for people to write books on
new and related subjects. If you have an idea for a book
please contact us at the above address.

This book may be purchased from the publisher.
Include $5.00 for shipping.
Please try your bookstore first.
You may write for a free catalog.

Schiffer Books are available at special discounts for bulk pur-
chases for sales promotions or premiums. Special editions, including personalized covers, corporate imprints, and excerpts
can be created in large quantities for special needs. For more
information contact the publisher:

In Europe, Schiffer books are distributed by
Bushwood Books
6 Marksbury Ave.
Kew Gardens
Surrey TW9 4JF England
Phone: 44 (0) 20 8392-8585; Fax: 44 (0) 20 8392-9876
E-mail: info@bushwoodbooks.co.uk
Website: www.bushwoodbooks.co.uk
Free postage in the U.K., Europe; air mail at cost.

Copyright © 2009 by Ballo Rebora
Library of Congress Control Number: 2008933698

Designed by RoS
Type set in Zapf Chancery Demi BT/Zurich BT

ISBN: 978-0-7643-3147-3
Printed in China

Dedication

First of all, I would like to dedicate this book to God, who blessed me by making me a father, a husband, a business man, and a proud woodcarver.

Following my first special dedication, I would also like to dedicate this book to both my Mother, Huicha, and my sister, Anita, for always encouraging the family to stay together and to fight for our own dreams.

Finally, I will also like to dedicate this book to my beloved wife, Guby, for her love and companionship along life's path.

Dedicatoria

Antes que nada quisiera dedicar este libro a Dios, quien hizo de mí a un Papa, un marido, un empresario y un orgulloso tallador de madera.

Siguiendo mi primera dedicatoria, también dedico este libro a Huicha y Anita por ser como son.

Finalmente también dedico este libro a mi amada esposa Guby, por su amor y compañía en este camino de la vida.

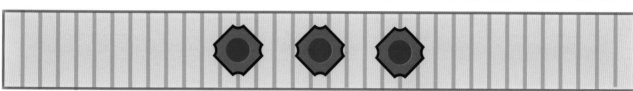

Contents

Sumario

Acknowledgments

Once again, and thank God I have been here and done this before, I am grateful for all the people who helped me in their own ways to make this book possible. I would like to first mention that this book was made possible by two wonderful people who keep on believing in the publishing possibilities of a book by and for woodcarvers. They have believed in my form of expression and my art. It is not easy to find people who are willing to take the joy and enthusiasms of a woodcarver, work as a team, and channel those into a published book. It is because of the good faith of Peter and Nancy Schiffer that I am able to write these Acknowledgments … and this book, *Carving a Mariachi Band* … at all.

I would like to thank all the people who smiled and agreed with the idea of making the Mariachi band the subject for this second book. Special mentions go to two great friends and artists , Meño Guzman and Rafa Lopez, from a little town named Tonala here in Mexico. They have taught me the art of looking at forms and colors in a really different way.

Thanks to Dave Stetson for his seminar and all that I learned from him. Dave gave me the self-confidence and the knowledge to make me feel much more secure in my carving.

Thanks again to my lovely wife, Guby, for keeping up her enthusiasm for my carving obsessions and for making this house a home in which to live.

I have to thank all the staff from Schiffer Publishing for making me feel like home every time I go for a carving mission in Atglen, Pennsylvania.

Special thanks to Ginger, Jeff, and Doug – these guys really know their jobs.

And, finally, I would like to thank all the carvers out there who enjoy the same passion as I do for this wonderful form of art that keeps us always with the daily satisfaction of carving a little more on our "Piece of Art" of the moment.

– Ballo Rebora

Agradecimientos

Una vez mas, y gracias a Dios eh estado aquí y hecho esto antes, Estoy muy agradecido con toda la gente que a su manera hicieron posible la realización de este libro. En primer lugar quiero mencionar que este libro es hoy una realidad gracias a dos personas increíbles que siempre han creído en las posibilidades sobre la publicación de libros de talladores y para talladores de madera. Ellos han creído en mí y en mi forma de expresión. No es fácil encontrar personas con esa capacidad para tomar este trabajo con tal entusiasmo y hacer un equipo para lograr un mismo fin. Estas dos maravillosas personas son Peter y Nancy Schiffer , todo mi agradecimiento.

Quisiera agradecer a todas las personas que les pareció buena idea hacer este segundo libro sobre el mariachi y me lo demostraban con una sonrisa.

Un agradecimiento especial quiero hacer a dos grandes amigos de Tonala Jalisco que me han enseñado a ver las formas y el color desde otro punto de vista, ellos son Meño Guzmán y Rafa López.

Agradezco también al maestro Dave Stetson por el seminario que tuve el honor de participar y en el cual adquirí una experiencia invaluable.

Agradezco nuevamente a mí amada esposa Guby por su entusiasmo y apoyo incondicional, por haber convertido una casa en un hogar.

Agradezco a todo el staff de Schiffer publishing en Atglen PA por ser tan amables con un servidor cada vez que eh ido en una mision de tallado.

Un agradecimiento muy especial para Ginger, Jeff y Doug, estos amigos si que saben su trabajo.

Finalmente agradezco a todos los talladores que comparten al igual que yo, el placer de tallar madera y siempre tienen a mano madera para seguir tallando.

– Ballo Rebora

Introduction

Prior to the arrival of Cortes the music of Mexico, played with rattles, drums, reed and clay flutes, and conch-shell horns, was an integral part of religious celebrations. Quickly, however, as Christianity spread along with the arriving Spaniards, while music remained essential to Mexican worship, in many areas the traditional instruments gave way to those imported by the Spanish: violins, guitars and harps, brass horns, and woodwinds.

Following this change in instruments, from these areas several of the most distinctive regional ensembles of Mexico developed, including the *Mariachi*.

Mariachi – What Does It Mean?

The explanation that appears most frequently – especially on record jackets and in travel brochures – is that *Mariachi* is a variation of the French word *mariage,* meaning wedding or marriage, and comes from the time in the nineteenth century when Maximillian, a Frenchman, was Emperor of Mexico. According to legend, the Mariachi bands were so named by the French after the celebration with which they were most commonly associated. Currently, however, the best scholarly opinion is that the word *mariachi* has native roots. But whatever its true source – and the truth may never be discovered with absolute certainty – the word today has one meaning that is crystal clear: *Mariachi* means one of the most exciting and enchanting musical ensembles found anywhere in the world. Their sound is the heart and soul of Mexico.

Although the origins of Mariachi music go back hundreds of years, in the form we know it, the Mariachi began in the nineteenth century in the Mexican state of Jalisco. My hometown of Guadalajara is located within the state of Jalisco.

By the 1930s, Mariachi musicians had begun wearing the *traje de charro*; this is the typical outfit that the Mexican Cowboys (*charros*) use. *La charreria* is the national sport and it is more or less a Mexican version of the Rodeo in the USA. The *traje de charro* consisting of a waist-length jacket and tightly fitted wool pants which open slightly at the ankle to fit over a short riding boot. Both pants and jacket are often ornamented with embroidery, intricately cut leather designs, or silver buttons in a variety of shapes. (The above text references Sylvia Gonzalez's *Mexico, the*

Introducción

Antes de la llegada de Cortes la música prehispánica en México era tocada con instrumentos autóctonos tales como, cascabeles, tambores, flautas de barro y caracoles gigantes, estos instrumentos autóctonos eran utilizados en ceremonias religiosas. Con la llegada de los españoles y la cristiandad llegaron a México los instrumentos europeos, violines, guitarras, arpas, trompetas de latón y flautas de madera.

Con este cambio en los instrumentos, México entro en una nueva era musical y empezaron a surgir diferentes manifestaciones musicales, entre ellas el Mariachi.

Mariachi-Que significa?

La explicación mas recurrente que aparece en libros, folletos y trípticos sobre el tema es que la palabra Mariachi se deriva de la palabra en francés mariage, que significa matrimonio, y según la leyenda esta palabra data del siglo diecinueve cuando Maximiliano era el emperador de México. Según esta leyenda, el Mariachi fue llamado: así dado que este tipo de música era asociada con las fiestas nupciales, sin embargo existen otras versiones en donde se cree que la palabra Mariachi tiene raíces nativas. Sea cual fuese la historia real y probablemente nunca la sabremos, lo que si es un hecho claro como el agua es que la palabra Mariachi hoy en dia simboliza una de las manifestaciones musicales mas autenticas a nivel mundial. El sonido del Mariachi es el corazón y alma del pueblo mexicano.

El origen del Mariachi data de cientos de años atrás, pero, el mariachi que hoy en dia se conoce se origino en el siglo diez y nueve en el estado de Jalisco. Guadalajara es la capital del estado de Jalisco, cuna de un servidor.

Desde los años treintas, los músicos de los mariachis han adoptado su vestimenta de traje de charro. La charrería es el deporte tradicionalmente nacional y consiste en una serie de suertes que tienen todo que ver con la vida de antaño del campo. El traje de charro consiste de pantalones de lana ajustados, un saco corto abierto y ambos decorados con ornamentos, botones y decoraciones en plata con diseños de diferentes formas.((El texto anterior esta basado en las referencias del escrito por Sylvia González: México, the meeting of Two Cultures (New York: Higgins and Associates, 1991.))

Meeting of Two Cultures (New York: Higgins and Associates, 1991.))

It did not take me long to decide on the subject for my second book on carving real traditions of Mexico. The Mariachi celebrate the great moments in the lives of the Mexican people. That is why I decided to carve this Mariachi band and show the world, in this unique art form (woodcarving), the typical characters that form an original Mariachi Band. I carve these mariachi members in a humorous way. Whenever I see a mariachi band playing, I have always the same characters, and now you will too! You will always find, in any Mariachi band, these typical icons: the fat guy, the thin guy, the old guy, all with thick mustaches … and some say they all use the same lotion… but most of all, when you experience the Mariachis, you always find the heart and soul of Mexico.

The five members that I carve represent an entertaining and engaging challenge for any woodcarver. Some of these Mariachis are a little bit harder to carve than others, with their original expressions and various instruments. But therein lie both the challenge and the fun. It is my great pleasure then to show this time *HOW TO CARVE A MARIACHI BAND*.

I will start with wood and pattern transfers, move on to the whole process of carving, and end with painting techniques.

Now it is time to start this wonderful journey. I wish all of you out there the most pleasant carving sessions of all….

– Ballo Rebora

No me fue difícil tomar el tema del Mariachi para hacer mi segundo libro de talla de madera sobre las tradiciones más características de México. El Mariachi celebra los grandes momentos en las vidas del pueblo mexicano. Es por ello que decidí tallar al Mariachi con sus miembros mas representativos y mostrar al mundo, en esta forma de arte (la talla de madera) los típicos miembros que lo conforman, claro, de una forma simpática y acentuando las características tan únicas de los mismos. Cada vez que veo a un Mariachi tocar, nunca faltan los mismos iconos tan característicos, El gordito, el flaco, el mas veterano, todos con grandes bigotes, en fin, hasta se podría decir que usan todos los miembros la misma loción. Cuando tengan la oportunidad de ver un mariachi tocando en vivo, entenderán esto que les comento y sentirán palpitar en ustedes todo el espíritu y alma del pueblo mexicano.

Los cinco integrantes que talle para este libro representan un reto divertido para cualquier tallador de madera. Algunos de ellos tienen un grado mayor de dificultad que otros, es ahí precisamente en donde estriba el reto y la diversión. Es por eso que con todo mi orgullo en esta ocasión doy un pequeño homenaje a todos los Mariachis de hoy y antaño con este libro de cómo tallar un Mariachi.

Empezare con los patrones y posteriormente todo el proceso y técnica de tallado y finalmente el pintado del mismo.

Es momento de empezar este maravilloso proceso. Les deseo de todo corazón las sesiones más placenteras de tallado…………

– Ballo Rebora

Tools

Here is a listing of all the tools needed to complete these projects successfully:

I use a variety of carving knives in this project. I recommend at least one good quality roughing knife and also at least one good quality detail knife.

Palm gouges are a helpful addition in this or any project. Most of the cuts made with these tools can be duplicated with a good knife.

Additional tools may make the carving process easier but are not necessary and, as always, you will learn your tools, and which additional tools are necessary, as the need arises.

I use sandpaper grit 150 and grit 80 to leave a smooth surface.

I use acrylic paint exclusively on my carvings. Specific colors for these projects are noted in the directions.

After the paint is dry I use Bee wax to seal the carving. Painting and finishing a woodcarving is an art. It requires practice, skill, and patience as everything else.

Herramientas

Aquí hay una lista de las herramientas necesarias para terminar estos proyectos exitosamente:

Yo utilizo diversas navajas para esculpir en este proyecto. Recomiendo al menos una navaja de desbaste de buena calidad y también al menos una buena navaja para detalles.

Más herramientas pueden hacer el proceso de labrado más sencillo, pero no son necesarias y, como siempre, usted conocerá sus herramientas y que herramientas adicionales requerirá, conforme se presente la necesidad.

Yo utilizo lija calibre 150 y 80 para dejar una superficie suave.

Utilizo exclusivamente pintura acrílica en mis esculturas. Los colores específicos para este proyecto están anotados en las instrucciones.

Una vez que la pintura haya secado utilice cera de abeja para sellar la escultura. Pintar y dar el terminado a un labrado en madera es todo un arte. Requiere de práctica, habilidad y paciencia como todo lo demás.

Sharp Tools

Carving with sharp tools is of the utmost importance in this art. Sharp tools make the difference. They not only produce better work, they also require less force to cut wood and they are, therefore, much safer for your hands.

Sharpening tools properly is an art in itself. I won't pretend to teach you something that I am still learning every day. For years I have been using a slipstrop to keep my knives in razor-like condition. After many years of stroping my knives, I have discovered a wonderful sharpening machine. I highly recommend it. It is the Ultimate Sharpener™ from Chipping Away. Along with this new machine, Pop, my good friend and owner of Chipping Away sent me this time the "Ultimate Power Honer"™ as well. This system has made my sharpening problems a thing from the past. Again, practice and experience will solve this issue for all of you and I am quite sure that you'll find the best way to accomplish this most important task.

Wood

When I started carving, many years ago, I used to carve with red oak. Somehow, in spite of the hardness of the wood, I managed to finish my carvings. In those days, I use to think that it was the best wood to carve, far better than pine.

I was introduced to basswood some years later. From that moment on, basswood has been my carving wood of choice. It is classified as a hard wood, but it is one of the softer hardwoods. Its even grain holds detail well, and it finishes smooth for painting. I get the best northern basswood from Smoky Mountain Woodcarvers Supply, Inc. at Nawger Nob.

There is something that I want to say, especially to the novices: There is not even one excuse … not the tools and knives, not the type of wood to use or anything else … to keep you from starting to carve. I am largely self-taught. Much of what I have learned in this incredible carving journey I have picked up along the way as needed. The will to carve was never been stopped or diminished by a lack of better wood or tools. So, if you have the desire to carve, just do it and life will take you into this incredible learning experience.

In this wonderful journey and, especially in the USA, there are many woodcarvers willing to assist you in this learning process. I have met two CCA (Caricature Carvers of America) members and attended their seminars. They are Dave Stetson and Tom Wolfe. I really recommend any carver, novice or expert, attend as many carving seminars as you can. You will always pick new tips and techniques on this wonderful art form and, most of all, you will meet friends with the same passion for this art.

Herramientas afiladas

Tallar con herramientas afiladas es de suprema importancia en este arte. Las herramientas afiladas hacen la diferencia. No sólo producen un mejor trabajo, sino también requieren de un menor esfuerzo para cortar la madera y son mucho más seguras para tus manos.

El dar un buen afilado a las herramientas es por si mismo un arte. No pretendo enseñarles algo de lo cual sigo aprendiendo día con día. Por años he estado utilizando un afilador SlipStrop (como el de los peluqueros de antaño) para mantener mis navajas afiladas. Tras muchos años de afilar con el SlipStrop mis navajas, he descubierto una maravillosa máquina para afilar. La recomiendo de manera importante. Es el Ultimate Sharpener ™ de Chipping Away. Pop, mi amigo y dueño de Chipping Away me hizo llegar una nueva maquina que complementa la primera, se llama la " Ultimate Power Honer" ™ Ha hecho de mis problemas de afilado algo del pasado. Nuevamente, la práctica y experiencia resolverán este asunto para todos ustedes y estoy seguro que con la práctica encontrarán la mejor manera de conseguir esta muy importante tarea.

Madera

Cuando empecé a esculpir hace muchos años solía tallar con cedro rojo. De alguna manera, en vista de la dureza de la madera, me las arreglé para terminar mis labrados. En aquellos días, solía pensar que esta madera era lo mejor para esculpir, al menos era mucho mejor que el pino.

Años mas tarde conocí el tilo (basswood). Desde entonces, el tilo (basswood) ha sido mi madera predilecta para tallar. Está clasificada como una madera dura, pero es una de las más suaves de este tipo. Su veta regular conserva adecuadamente los detalles, y se termina suavemente para su pintado. Yo consigo el mejor tilo del norte de Smoky Mountain Woodcarvers Supply, Inc. en Nawger Nob TN USA.

Hay algo que quiero decir, en especial a los novatos: No existen excusas… ni las herramientas ni las navajas, ni el tipo de madera a utilizar para desanimarte a iniciar a esculpir. Yo soy autodidacta. Todo lo que he aprendido en este formidable viaje de la talla de madera lo he aprendido a lo largo del camino. El deseo de esculpir jamás se ha detenido o disminuido por falta de una mejor madera o mejores herramientas. Por lo tanto, si tienen el deseo de esculpir, simplemente háganlo, la vida los llevará hacia esta increíble experiencia de aprendizaje.

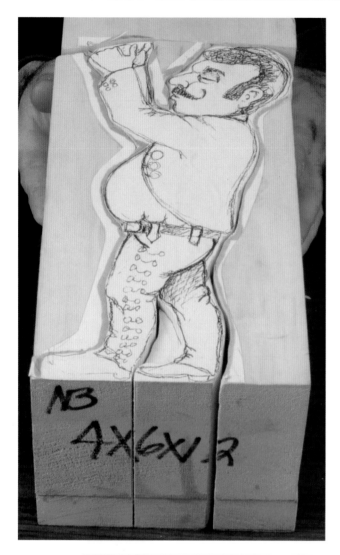

The wood to be used in this project is northern basswood. This basswood is grown in southern Canada and the northern United States. This basswood comes in blocks measuring 4" x 6" x 12" Given these measurements, for this project I glued two basswood blocks together and trimmed them to create a block measuring 5" x 6" x 12".

Once the block is glued and dried, cut and paste a copy of the Mariachi pattern to the block.

La Madera que utilicé es basswood Americano, esta Madera crece en el sur de Canadá y el norte de Estados Unidos. Esta madera es cortada en bloques de 4" x 6" x 12" pulgadas, en este caso ensamble una pulgada extra de la misma madera cuidando la orientación de la beta para obtener un grosor de 5" pulgadas.

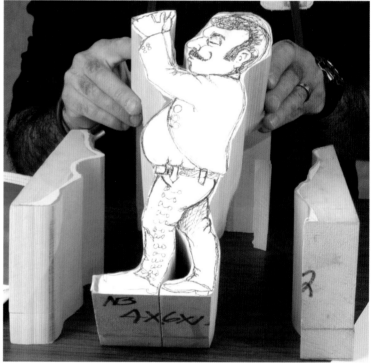

Cut out around the pattern with the band saw, removing excess wood.

Corte alrededor de la plantilla con la sierra banda.

Use calipers to accurately measure the depth of the block and find the middle of the block's side.

Utilice calibradores o pie de rey para determinar la línea central lateral y frontal.

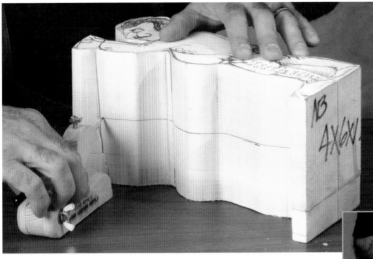

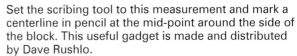

Set the scribing tool to this measurement and mark a centerline in pencil at the mid-point around the side of the block. This useful gadget is made and distributed by Dave Rushlo.

As you can see, we are using carving knives and roughing gouges (made by Warren) and a roughing knife designed to remove large chunks of wood during the early roughing out of the figure.

En este caso utilicé un instrumento llamado scribing tool de mi gran amigo Dave Rushlo para ayudarme a rayar el bloque con medidas idénticas.
Utilizo una gurbia ancha y semi plana para remover grandes pedazos de madera en este proceso inicial de desbaste.

We start rough-ing out the block at the head, removing the ex-cess basswood stock.

Empezamos des-bastando el área de la cabeza para que se empiece a definir.

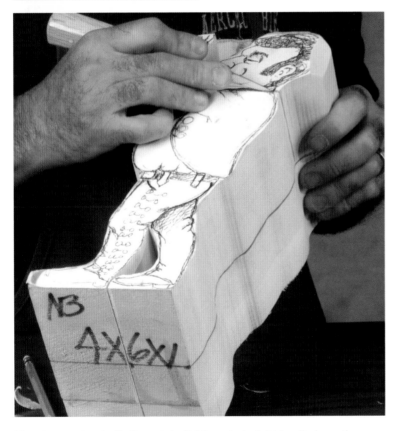

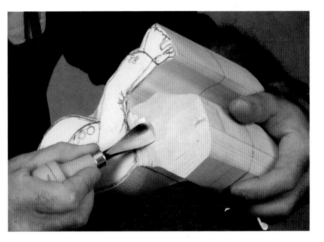

We use the best tool available to narrow the head, in this case a Warren wide 3/4 fixed handle gouge, to about 3/5 of the original size. This is a slow process, carefully removing excess wood. Just a word about the tools I use. I am using tools that I have learned from experience work for me. They may not be the same tools that work best for you. Over time you will determine which tools are most useful to you for each step of the carving. So consider the tools I mention to be informed suggestions of what may work well for you. They are a place to start but are recommenda-tions rather than decrees.

Es importante entender que las herramientas que uti-lice son simplemente las que en su momento y dada la tarea a realizar, me dan a mi el mejor resultado, cada quien debe aprender y seleccionar la herramien-ta ya sea navaja o gurbia que mejor les funcione en determinada tarea. En este caso, esta gurbia ancha, semi plana y manual es bastante efectiva.

Use the carving knife (bench knife) to cut straight in all along the neckline to make a stop cut. This will make rounding down the head easier as it will keep the knife from slipping down into the shoulder area while carving away excess stock.

Con una navaja de desbaste, marqué la línea divisoria de la cabeza y el cuello para evitar cortar los hombros, empiece a definir esta área y sus volúmenes.

I use calipers to repeatedly check the diminishing dimensions of the head. Place marks at the proper size of the head. This is important, as you can't put wood back if you cut off too much.

Utilizo el pie de rey constantemente para revisar las dimensiones de la cabeza, marque puntos de referencia.

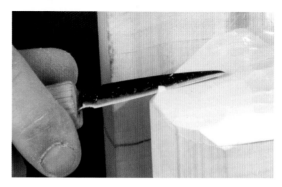

This is a good knife for roughing.

Esta es una magnifica navaja de desbaste.

Start to separate the two arms by making a stop cut with your bench knife. This stop cut acts as a guide to start chipping with the knife and gouge. Remember as you reduce excess stock that everything is to be more or less symmetrical.

Empiece a separar ambos brazos marcando un corte de paro recto y profundo verticalmente. Recuerde siempre mantener la simetría entre ambos miembros.

I am using a #3 sweep, which is 1/2" wide gouge, to separate the arms. We have separated the arms at this point.

Utilizo esta herramienta para esta tarea de separar los brazos. Los brazos han sido separados.

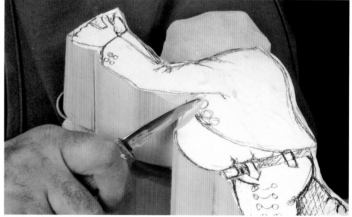

Make a stop cut under the arm to start to separate the raised arm from the belly.

Haga un corte de paro bajo el brazo para separar la panza del brazo.

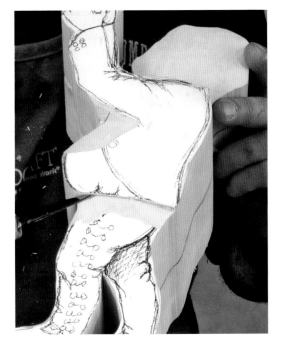

Mark the bottom of the belly so we don't miss that line while carving. Once we have the stop cut at the belly, we need to start to cut out the forward positioned left leg. Make a stop cut here following the line of the leg. Start to remove excess wood from the leg. We take out all this part, more of less. As you can see, the pattern is being carved away as we work. I always make at least 5 copies of the pattern to work with as the initial copy glued to the block gets carved away.

Marque la línea horizontal de la panza para determinarla. Una vez trazada esta línea comenzamos a trabajar en la pierna que se adelanta en esta posición, desbastando la madera que tiene que ser removida completamente, tome unos minutos y revise su patrón o plantilla para entender los cortes. Afile sus navajas y gurbias cada vez que sea necesario, recuerde que el filo de las herramientas es primordial para obtener resultados.

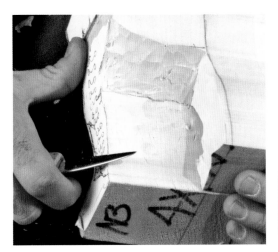

The excess wood has been cut away from the back of the leg right up to the block's center-line.

El exceso de Madera a sido removida obteniendo obteniendo este resultado,

> STOP FREQUENTLY TO SHARPEN YOUR TOOLS. THIS WILL MAKE CARVING EASIER, MORE ENJOYABLE, AND SAFER AS YOU WILL HAVE BETTER CONTROL OVER YOUR TOOLS.

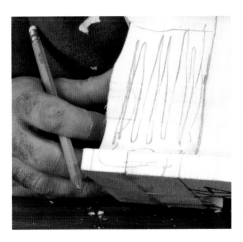
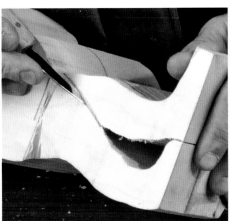

Now we will work on the back positioned right leg, the leg that is pulled back to steady the Mariachi as he plays. Here the excess stock that must be removed is shown darkened with pencil. Make a stop cut along the pattern line indicating the front of the thigh and begin removing excess wood with a gouge, cutting toward the stop cut line.

Es momento de trabajar en la pierna que pisa más atrás, y que nivela el movimiento del mariachi tocando la trompeta. Se muestra obscurecida a lápiz la parte a ser removida con navaja o gurbia. Marque con un corte profundo la zona a delimitar para terminar esta labor tallando.

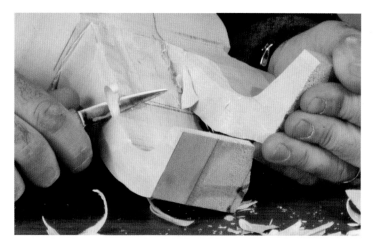

Now that we have two legs, we cannot make a mistake and cut the wrong part. I take pictures of a willing assistant in the mariachi's stance from 4 directions to act as a model for me and to see the proper stance my mariachi should take. If people you know are camera shy, ask someone to take four pictures of you and be your own model! Start rounding the corners symmetrically all around the legs …

Ahora debemos tener mucho cuidado al eliminar la parte extra de cada una de las piernas, no podemos cortar mal… tómese cinco minutos para entender lo que esta próximo a hacer y empiece cortando rebanadas firmes pero delgadas. Si necesita un modelo de tercera dimensión, mírese a usted mismo en dicha posición, finalmente es una personita con las mismas características físicas que cualquiera. Redondee las esquinas de las piernas con cuidado con una navaja mediana.

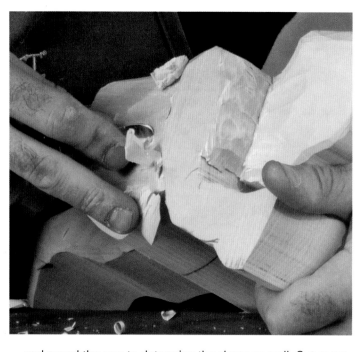

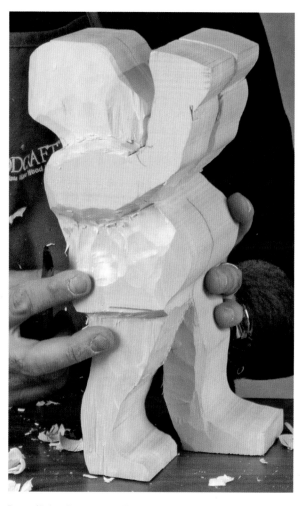

… and round the arm to determine the shape as well. Cut away at the belly after shaping the arm.

Igualmente, redondee los brazos en general, vaya tallando ambos brazos y ambas piernas de una manera simétrica para que la proporción vaya aflorando y resulte en automático.

Round the figure carefully to keep the figure evenly carved.

Redondee la pieza para mantener el equilibrio simétrico en disminución proporcional.

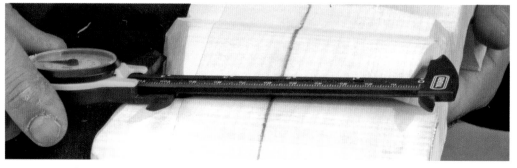

Measure to find the center of the figure to make sure you keep the figure properly balanced.

Mida constantemente la línea central de la pieza para mantener la proporción adecuada.

While rounding the arms, we need to make room between the arms to make room for the lower part of the face.

Mientras tallamos los antebrazos, debemos de hacer espacio en medio de ambos brazos para la cara inferior (boca, cachetes y piocha.)

Cut through the excess wood between the arms to the face. Round the arms to get a better perspective of this area. Round the arms and the legs. Keep turning the piece to assure even work. Periodically take measurement from the pattern to assure that you don't cut off too much. Cut a little from the top of the belly to get rid of the marks from the band saw.

Perfore de lado a lado el área de los brazos intermedia que tiene que ser removida para poder trabajar posteriormente en la cara inferior, prosiga redondeando los brazos y las piernas simétricamente y analice el patrón o plantilla del mariachi trompetista y rectifique. Rasure suavemente con su navaja de detalle la panza, asegurando una vista suave y natural de la barriga en redondo.

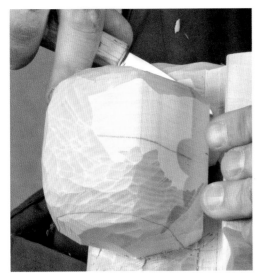

Now that we have carved away excess wood and can see the area that will be the face, we may start rounding down the head.

Ahora que tallamos lo suficiente y podemos ver el área que será la cara, podemos empezar redondeando la cabeza.

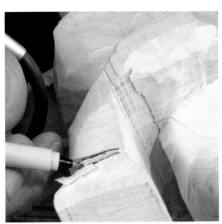

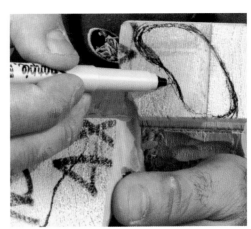

Mark the arm below the hand at the shirtsleeve cuff.

Marque la separación de la mano y la manga claramente con sus respectivos niveles.

Use your bench knife to place a stop cut line along the line where the back of the shirt and jacket meet the back of the pants.

Usa tu navaja para marcar y definir el área que separa la parte trasera baja de la camisa y la chamarra con la parte alta de los pantalones.

Determine the Mariachi's footprint. His shoe size will give you a feel for the proper size of the leg.

Trace la plantilla del zapato por la parte inferior del pie y empiece a tallar el zapato, esto le dará sentido de proporción a la pierna en conjunto.

Start to carefully carve away at the excess wood around the foot. Don't carve away too much just yet. This is an early rounding stage.

Empiece a tallar el zapato lentamente, esto es un PRE tallado final por lo que debemos tener cuidado de no tallar de mas.

Keep looking at you piece make sure the proportions are correct while you continue rounding and narrowing the legs down toward proper proportions. Follow the grain of the wood to keep your carving tools from digging in too deep.

Como siempre, siga observando detenidamente su pieza, rectifique errores, ahora es cuando!!! Sigue la ruta de la beta de la madera, profundizando poco a poco y cuidando nuestras navajas de no enterrarse demasiado.

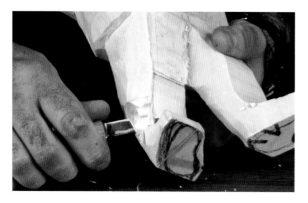 

Keep in mind that the leg grows narrower toward the foot. In your mind's eye you should see the leg and remove the wood to get to that imagined leg.

Recuerda que la pierna va de mas ancha a mas delgada de arriba a bajo, recuerde esa imagen mental y talle las piernas del mariachi de igual forma.

As you get closer to the actual size of the figure, you need to remove smaller pieces and work slowly; the Mariachi takes shape. You might say at this point that we are cleaning the piece up.

Mientras mas tallemos la pieza mas cerca estaremos de llegar a las proporciones deseadas , es por esto que debemos tallar con mas cuidado y no tallar de mas, es momento de concentrarnos en la imagen final deseada del individuo que se este tallando.

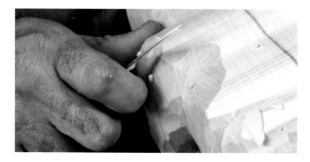 

I am working to remove the square, block shape from the body. Working toward, and with reference to, the centerline. You always keep that centerline intact to maintain balance in the piece.

Estoy trabajando en hacer un tanto menos cuadrado el cuerpo en si del Mariachi, lo veo un tanto cuadrado....conserve la línea central para referencia del balance de la pieza.

Carving a little at a time to reveal the figure. Note that the pants have now been separated and reduced away from the back of the shirt and jacket.

Tallando poco a poco la pieza va apareciendo. Observe como los pantalones han sido separados y reducidos de la parte trasera de la camisa y chamarra.

The rounded figure to this point. When you reach this stage, it will be time to work on the jacket.

La pieza tallada y redondeada hasta el momento, Es momento de trabajar en la chamarra.

Draw in the outline of the jacket and make a stop cut straight down along the pencil line of that jacket.

Dibuje y trace rebanando la línea de la chamarra con la punta de la navaja, profundo para denotar la chamarra.

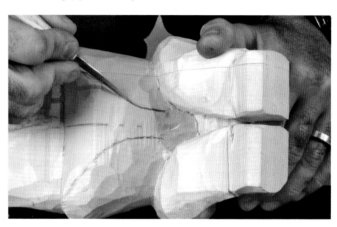

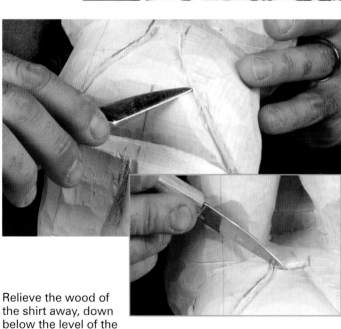

Relieve the wood of the shirt away, down below the level of the jacket, to raise the jacket above the shirt using a bench knife. As the jacket takes shape, clean up the form and make sure to leave some extra wood here for the necktie.

Resaque la Madera de la camisa respetando las Alturas y niveles de los balcones de Madera. Respete el montículo de donde saldrá el moño en el pecho sobre la camisa y en medio del cuello y la caída de la chamarra.

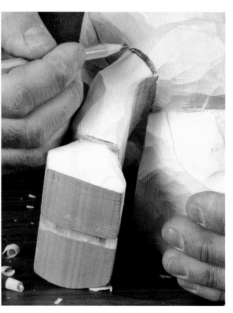

To begin carving the face, first mark a guideline for the band saw across the arms at the point where the arms meet the body.

Es momento de determinar la línea por donde pasara la sierra banda, amputando los brazos para poder trabajar la cara y rostro y finalmente re-ensamblar pegando los brazos.

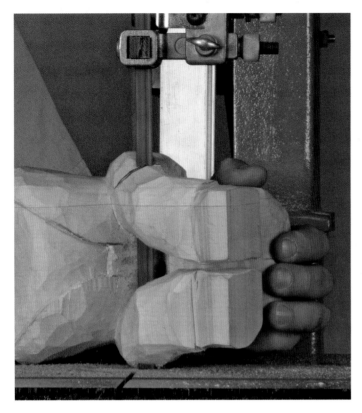

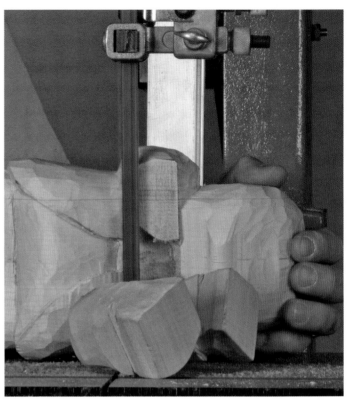

Be very careful not to cut into the face as you cut off the arms with the band saw. The band saw blade is threaded into the gap between the face and the arms. This way you cut away from the head and do not risk decapitating your Mariachi.

Tenga cuidado de no cortar parte de la cara al amputar los brazos con la sierra banda, La sierra se acomoda entre el centro del espacio cara-brazos para asegurar no cortar de mas. Decapitar al amigo....

A terrible scene … but one that will be repaired later! The arms have been cleanly removed. The area of the face is now exposed for easy carving.

Esta es una escena espantosa!!! Estará bien al final, no se preocupen, fue una amputación exitosa…Ahora si podemos tallar la cara libremente. Nada nos lo dificulta más de lo normal.

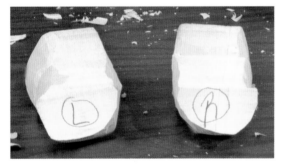

I mark the arms left and right so I don't make a mistake and take a little wood away that I should not to make sure the arms match up properly when they are reattached.

Señale Con un plumón los brazos para no confundirse y coincidan en el momento del ensamble.

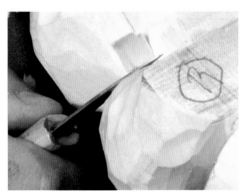

Beginning to round down the head with the bench knife.

Empiezo a redondear la cabeza con una Buena navaja.

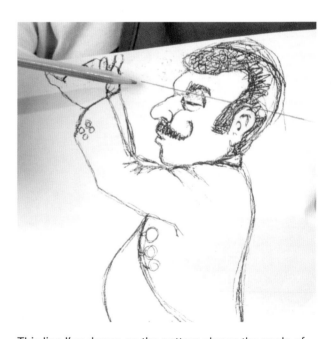

This line I've drawn on the pattern shows the angle of the face. This guy is going to have his face tilted up while playing an upraised trumpet. The face we will carve is a little bit like a triangle with the base at the top and the point at the chin.

Esta línea que trace marca el ángulo de la cabeza, el tocara la trompeta mirando a lo alto, La cara a tallar deberá de tener una forma lógica.

16

Take the measurements of the head and shoulders to see how much excess wood needs to be taken off.

Tome y verifique las medidas de la cabeza y los hombros para estimar que tanta Madera será desvastada.

We need to narrow the arms and shoulders at this point to keep things in proportion.

Debemos adelgazar los brazos un poco más para mantener las proporciones.

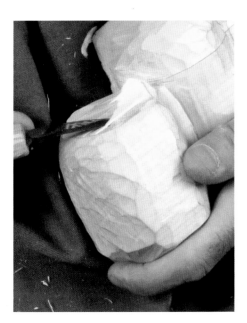

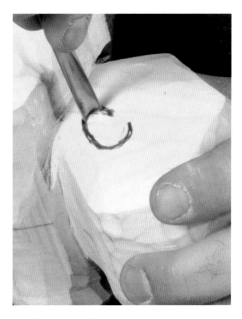

Removing excess wood from the head.

Rebanando mas Madera de la cabeza que sobra....

Once the head is the right size, leaving enough wood for hair, facial features, and ears, draw in the ears.

Una vez que la cabeza adquiere su tamaño deseado con volumen suficiente para el cabello, facciones de la cara, orejas, trace el contorno de las orejas.

Position this #8 sweep gouge to make a stop cut for the lobe of the ear.

Coloque esta gurbia en este sitio para crear el lóbulo de la oreja.

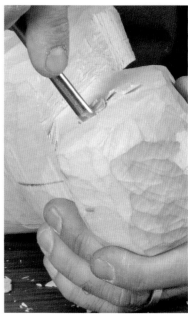

Use a bench knife to relieve the head away from around the outside of the ear, raising the ear a bit above the side of the head. Use a small U gouge to create the hollow of the inner ear. As you rough out the ears, use your calipers to check the proper ear size from the pattern against the ear carving to ensure the size remains right.

Utilizo una navaja de detalle mediana para resaltar las orejas de la cara, separación de los pisos y niveles. Utilizo una gurbia en u pequeña para crear el orificio auditivo y su contorno. Mida con el pie de rey el tamaño de la oreja del patrón o plantilla y verifique sus medidas en el Mariachi en cuestión.

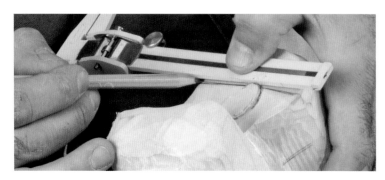
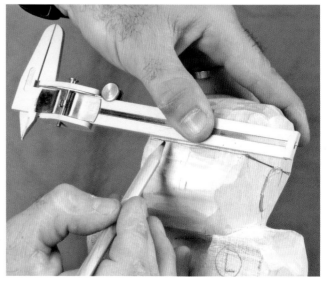

We must make a line to determine the eyebrows' relation to the ear. The eyebrows lie along the same line as the tops of the ears. This line should be drawn around the whole head.

Necesitamos trazar una línea horizontal en las cejas para determinar la correcta relación
Con la parte inferior de la oreja.

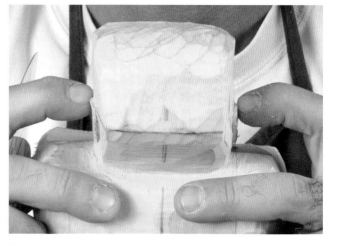

Now rough out the big ears a little more.

Resaque más las orejotas, un poco mas, es un Oregón....

Now that we have the ears here, we are going to start making the nose. We have the side of the head carved; now we need the front plane.

Dejamos a un lado las orejas y nos concentramos en la nariz. Tenemos los laterales de la cabeza tallados, es momento de hacer el plano frontal de la cara.

The egg-shaped head is divided in three equal parts horizontally. Draw in the horizontal dividing lines all around the head. Also draw in a centerline from top to bottom as an additional guide. Along the top horizontal line the eyebrows and tops of the ears are aligned. The bottom of the nose rests on the second horizontal line. The mouth is centered along the bottom horizontal line.

La cabeza semeja la forma de un huevo, divídalo en tres partes iguales horizontales a lo Redondo. Trace la línea central vertical que divide la cara en dos hemisferios. En la línea mas alta empiezan las cejas y las puntas inferiores de las orejas, la parte baja de la nariz descansa en la segunda línea horizontal. La boca esta al centro de la tercera línea, entre la parte baja de la nariz y la piocha.

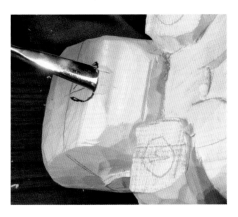

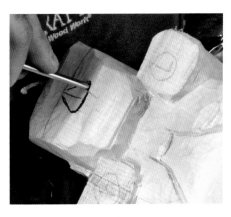

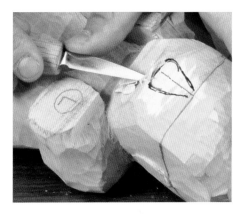

Make the stop cut with the 12 mm or 1/2" sweep gouge at the base of the nose.

Corta de manera vertical con una gurbia chica plana o navaja la base de la nariz.

Then with the #8 sweep 5/16"/8mm gouge for the nostrils.

Con una gurbia en u pequeña resaque los orificios nasales, que se noten…

Use a bench knife to relieve wood away from beneath the stop cut at the base of the nose.

Con una navaja de detalle limpie las marcas y Remarque la nariz para hacer más dramático el detalle de las facciones faciales.

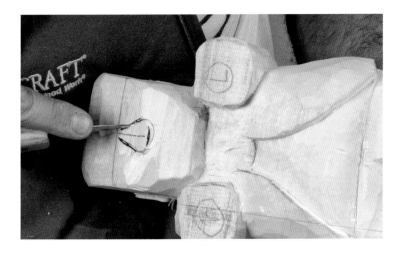

Make a stop cut along the sides of the nose and keep relieving excess wood away from the nose, carving up to that stop cut lines.

Talle los laterales de la nariz para proporcionarla y que aparezca, cortando hacia los cortes previos.

Continue to relieve wood away from the nose and the nostrils. Keep repeating the process, reestablishing your cut lines as you carve, and the nose will slowly emerge. As you can see from my photo, the nose covers half of the area of the face. So you keep relieving the outline of the nose, you should be mindful to leave enough wood for the cheeks. This is a good time to stop to sharpen your bench knife. Be careful not carve away too much from beneath the nose as you will need extra wood there to carve the Mariachi's mustache.

Continúe tallando la nariz y su forma deseada junto con los alerones nasales externos, estos tienen un volumen extra en Madera,

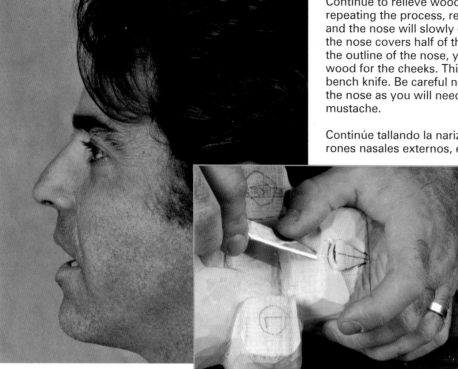

talle la forma de la nariz despacio, con mucho cuidado de dejar suficiente Madera donde se requiera, deje suficiente madera a los lados de los laterales nasales para los cachetes que en este caso serán bastante grandes…
Es momento de afilar nuestras navajas y gurbias, recuerde, una navaja bien afilada hace la diferencia. Recuerde dejar suficiente madera bajo la nariz para el súper bigote…

See how I have begun to define the cheekbones as I carve excess wood away from the nose. Note how the nose is raising above the rest of the face. I am also relieving excess wood away from the eyebrows and creating the hollows the eyes will be set into.

Observe como eh dejado suficiente madera para los cachetes y resaltando la nariz al mismo tiempo. Observe que la nariz es la parte más alta de la cara, Es momento de empezar a hacer las medias naranjas para los ojos, los ojos en si.

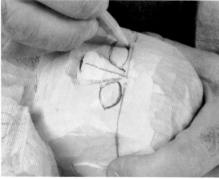

Now we have cleared some volume to draw on the eye. With the detail knife you can carve inside the eye pattern lines to begin to round out the eyes, like a half of a lemon as you can see from the pattern drawing. To begin carving the curve of the eye, first cut a stop cut line straight in around the inside of the eye pattern lines. Then begin carving from the center of the eye out toward the stop cut lines, rounding the surface with the highest point at the center of the eye. The eye is relieved below the edges of the eye pattern lines, which become the eyelids.

He creado un volumen suficiente en forma de media naranja para los ojos, puedo trazar los parpados en estos volúmenes oculares. Con la punta de la navaja corte una línea rodeando el ojo y resacando el párpado superior, Haga lo mismo en el párpado inferior, con la navaja de detalle profundice y aplane este corte para que se marquen claramente los parparos y en el centro espacio suficiente para la pupila.

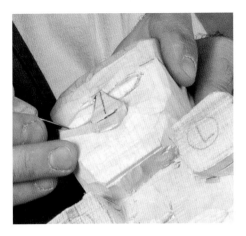
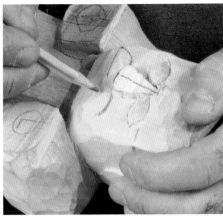
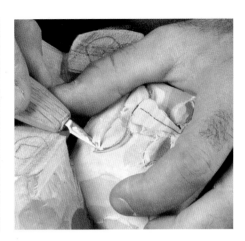

Take your time. Repeat the cuts, first cutting more deeply around the edges and then "shaving" wood lightly from the centers outward toward the deepening edges to achieve to correct shape of the spherical eyes within its lids.

Tome su tiempo. Repita el corte varias veces, poco a poco hasta que se profundice lo necesario para que bote el pedacito de Madera y quede el corte siguiendo la línea esférica del corte.

Trace in the mustache. All the Mariachi band members have the mustache!

Trace el bigote. Todos los miembros del Mariachi usan bigote con mucho orgullo!

Make your stop cuts around the edge of the mustache. Then relieve excess wood away from around the mustache, raising the mustache above the rest of the face.

Delimite con cortes firmes al rededor del bigote para que este predomine en la cara, Es un bigotón…

The face is the most challenging part of this carving. To get the face right takes time and care. If you feel you are getting stressed, move away from the face and relax by carving the legs, arms, or shoes and return to the face later when you are relaxed to avoid making unnecessary mistakes. After all, carving should be fun!

La cara es la parte mas difícil de esta talla. Hacer una cara bien hecha toma tiempo y cuidado. Si siente que se esta estresando, ya sabe que hacer, concéntrese en otra parte del cuerpo, piernas, brazos o los zapatos quizá, regrese a la cara en otro momento y seguramente lo vera mas claro. Después de todo, tallar se trata de gozar!

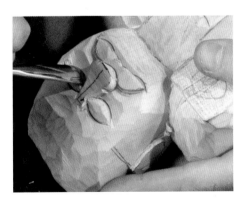
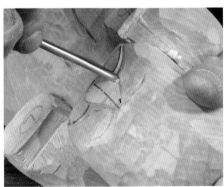

Now begin to round down the head, taking away excess wood and emphasizing the features. Be sure to remove all the sharp corners, as human faces don't have them. This will really change this guy's look. Don't forget to deepen the nostrils and remove excess material from around the cheeks. Refer to the pattern drawings frequently as you work. Take your time. It is very important to deepen the facial features in order to make them more prominent since this guy is a fat guy.

Continuamos disminuyendo la cabeza y enfatizando las facciones. Asegúrese de rasurar todas las orillas cuadradas de la cara, una cara humana no tiene orillas, Esto realmente cambiara la imagen de este hombre. No olvide tallar los orificios nasales profundos y los laterales nasales que se noten. Revise constantemente la plantilla o patrón para referencia. Es muy importante que las facciones sean las de una persona obesa, es un gordo este Mariachero.

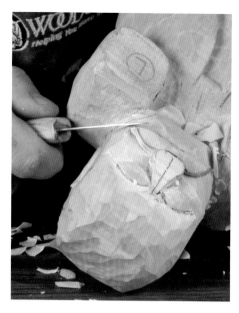  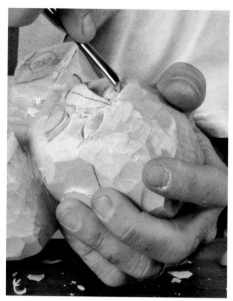

I am removing excess wood from the area of the cheeks.

Tallo dando forma aun mas el área de los cachetes.

This Mariachi is a little pop-eyed. Use a detail knife and small sweep gouges to flatten the eyes a bit and to deepen the areas around the lids to provide separation between the lids and eyes themselves. You need to carve the eyes very deeply in order to clearly separate the lids from the eyeball. The lid should add to the round appearance of the eyeball.

Este Mariachi es ojo saltado y gordo. Con la navaja de detalle y una gurbia semi plana muy pequeña talle entre el parpado y el ojo para separar claramente estos elementos. Es necesario profundizar estos cortes para separar claramente el parpado del ojo. El parpado debe abrazar la esfera ocular.

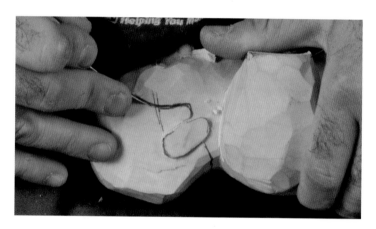

Now is the time to carve the sideburns and define the hair. Trace the pattern outline of the hair and sideburns around the head. Make a stop cut along the hairline.

Es momento de tallar las patillas y definir el cabello en general. Trace el contorno con lápiz, el corte de cabello deseado y las patillas. Haga un corte de aproximadamente 2 mm de profundidad sobre la línea y resaque. (stop cut)

Use your bench knife to make steep, shallow cuts with the knife tip, virtually parallel to the sides of the head back from the forehead toward the stop cut lines of the sideburns and hairline, slowly relieving the forehead below the level of the hairline.

Con cortes angulados con la punta de la navaja presente la línea del cabello y el contorno de las patillas, mostrando así poco a poco la frente. Evalúe la profundidad de la frente considerando las cejas.

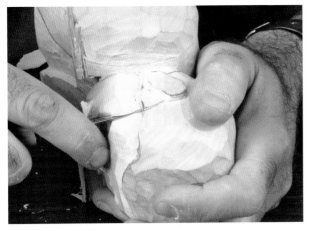

If you turn your head, you see that the eyeball sticks out a little out on the side of your face. By making little V cuts here along the side of the face with the bench knife, we imitate that feature, exposing the eye along the side of the face a bit, imitating the shape of the bone of the eye socket.

Si nos observamos de lado, veremos que la pelota del ojo es perfectamente visible. Imitamos esa misma forma en nuestra talla y en la orilla exterior del ojo salen pequeñas arrugas o las famosas arrugas llamadas "pata de gallo", con pequeños cortes hacemos estas arrugas. La forma del hueco ocular del cráneo es imitada lo más posible.

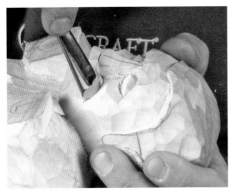

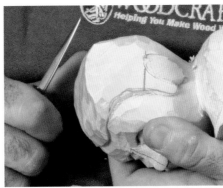

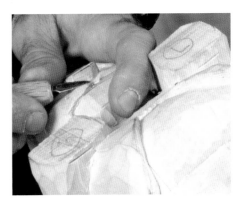

Continue defining the cheeks and mustache. I'm using a shallow gouge to refine the shape of the mustache and make the cheeks more prominent. The shallow gouge works well to round this area.

Continúe definiendo los cachetes y el bigote, utilice una gurbia semi plana pequeña para definir limpiamente estas partes., esta gurbia es efectiva para esta tarea.

Use the bench knife now to round the head, taking away sharp corners and flat surfaces.

Utilice la navaja para redondear la cabeza, rasurando esquinas y áreas planas.

Using the bench knife to trimming the edges of the mustache, rounding the sharp, square edges to make them appear more natural.

Rasurando orillas del bigote levemente, Dando una apariencia y limpieza más natural al tallado.

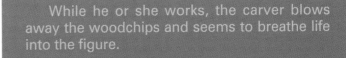

While he or she works, the carver blows away the woodchips and seems to breathe life into the figure.

Mientras tallamos, el escultor elimina pedacitos de Madera y pareciera que la figura empezara a respirar vida.

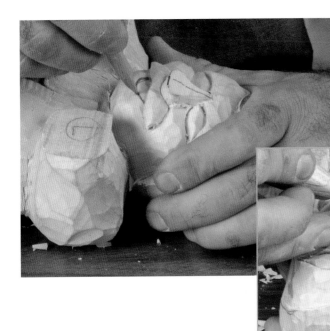

To make the lower lip, draw in the lower lip pattern line first. Use the bench knife to cut straight in along the pattern line of the lower lip to create a stop cut. Note the progress of the facial features at this point.

Para hacer el labio inferior, dibuje primero el trazo con lápiz del mismo.

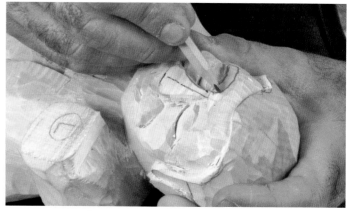

Steeply angle the knife to get the chin to show. Makes sure to cut deeply with the point of the knife, cutting at the correct angle to reveal that chin.

Profundice el ángulo de ataque de la navaja para resaltar la barbilla. Asegúrese de profundizar la punta de su navaja, cortando en el ángulo correcto.

Now we can draw the eyebrows. Note I have draw in a centerline down the nose to help in the proper and symmetrical placement of the eyebrows.

Es tiempo de trazar a lápiz las cejas. Note la línea central que nos ayuda a posicionar las cejas.

Start to round the nose using the detail knife with a paring action. Round down all the sharp edges, including at the base of the nose and nostrils.

Redondee la nariz con su navaja de detalle con movimientos circulares simetricos. Redondee todas las esquinas eh inperfecciones visibles.

As you carve, work in the round (or "round robin" one might say), moving first here and then there. By constantly moving from place to place, you keep the carving even. By changing the angles, you see new areas that need work, removing rough edges and sharp angles as you rotate the piece.

Modele y redondee la nariz con su navaja de detalle, rasure las orillas o cuadraturas que encuentre, atacando toda la pieza y observándola detenidamente para mantener una paridad de ambos lados del cuerpo. Al manipular la pieza en todas direcciones nos permite detectar detalles a corregir, pareciera que saltan a la vista cada vez más claros.

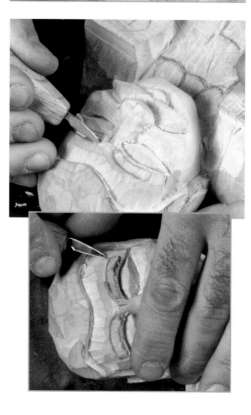

Now we are going to carve the eyebrows. Make the stop cut on the pattern line. With the skill of the surgeon I carefully remove a little bit at a time, relieving the forehead away from the eyebrows, raising them above the face.

Ahora tallaremos las cejas. Haga el Stop cut en la línea trazada con el lápiz, con un pulso de cirujano, corto suavemente, repetidamente sobre el mismo corte hasta que separe la frente y las cejas. Las cejas sobresalen de la cara.

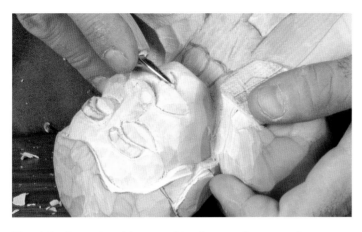

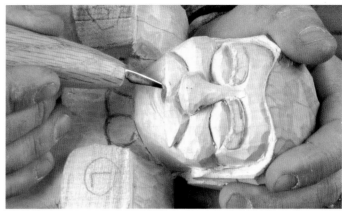

Blend the lip to the chin, round it, alternate between the sweep gouge and the detail knife as needed. Shaving tiny pieces off one at a time.

Funda el labio inferior a la barbilla, alterne su herramienta hasta encontrar la adecuada. Rasure poco a poco con precaución.

Create the tiny hollow in the center of the lower lip to make the mouth appear puckered so the Mariachi can toot his own horn.

Es momento de hacer un hueco en el centro de la boca para simular que sopla su instrumento y sentar la boquilla de la trompeta.

Now we are going to carve the hair. You need these three gouges: one large, one small, and one in the middle. They are called sweep gouges. The big one is #11 or 7/16" or 11 mm in size. The mid-sized sweep is 3/16 and the smallest gouge is 1/16, more or less.

Ahora tallaremos la cabellera. Para mejores resultados es necesario utilizar tres gurbias en u de tres tamaños 7/16 mm, 3/16 y 1/16. La idea es hacer surcos con la gurbia más gruesa ondulados y en el interior de estos, hacer surcos más delgados creando una vista más natural del cabello.

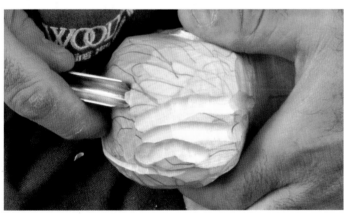

They say that the hair grows from the front to the back. So I am drawing hair guidelines in pencil first forward and then back. As you want the hair to move, you move the tools in a sweeping motion. Make sure you don't cut yourself in the process. Begin by working with the large gouge to make the general outlines of the sweep of the hair. The next size tool is used right in the middle of the area cut with the large gouge to add depth.
Don't concentrate on one spot. Always keep returning to other parts of the head as you carve. While we are here, shape the neck, gradually bringing it in to the right dimension. If the hair becomes too uneven you can shave some off to bring it back to the right look.

El cabello crece de la parte frontal hacia atrás. Trazo con lápiz las guías de la caída del cabello de una manera ondulada, una vez trazadas estas líneas guías, con la gurbia mas gruesa sígalas y posteriormente recorra el mismo camino con la gurbia que le sigue en tamaño menor y finalmente termine con la gurbia mas pequeña realzando las cúspides de las cordilleras para añadir profundidad. Haga esto en toda la cabellera para dar una apariencia de volumen y movilidad. Mientras estamos en este punto, puede empezar a determinar mas claramente el cuello, si el cabello resulta largo es momento de hacer el corte adecuado del mismo.

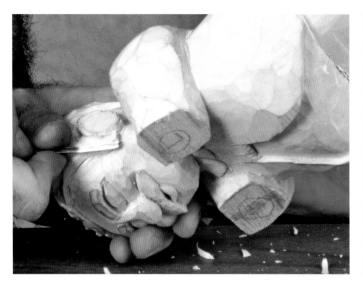

Using the smallest sweep, blending the sideburns to the face.

Utilizo una gurbia pequeña para fundir y limpiar discretamente las patillas y la cara.

Trim in front of the ear so the ear will be at a lower plane right behind the sideburn. This allows the ear to angle down into the side of the head behind the sideburn.

La parte frontal de la oreja es mas baja que la patilla, la oreja toma un ángulo descendente hacia la parte lateral trasera de la patilla.

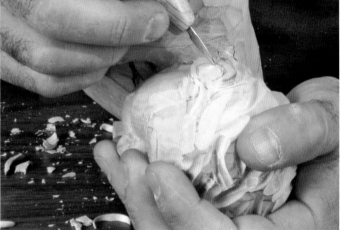

Make a little notch with this small gouge to begin cleaning up the ear by establishing the location of the ear canal. Then draw a line for the inner edge of the ear. Make a stop cut on that line and chip out the inner area of the ear down toward the canal. Then you can round the outer edge of the ear.

Haga un pequeño orificio auditivo con la gurbia pequeña, trace y talle la parte interior de la oreja haciendo un corte circular y tallando en ángulo descendiente hasta llegar al lóbulo interior, Las orejas son diferentes todas pero tienen una misma característica interior, estúdiela. Redondee la parte externa de la misma.

Undercut the bottom edge of the ear to create the lobe.

Corte por la parte de abajo de la oreja para mostrar el lóbulo inferior de la oreja.

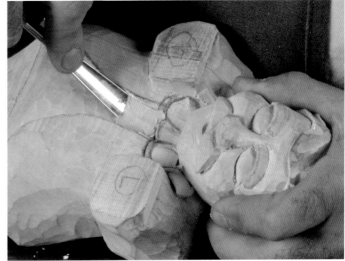

Make the stop cuts around the bowtie. Then chip at the front and side to bring the bowtie out. Use the point of the knife at an angle to work your way around the edge and chipping away little pieces of wood in a controlled fashion to reveal the bowtie.

Es momento de hacer el moño. Marque con corte profundo el contorno del mismo y con un stop-cut retire las orillas de este volumen poco a poco para presentar claramente el moño, Este deberá sobresalir del chaleco y la camisa.

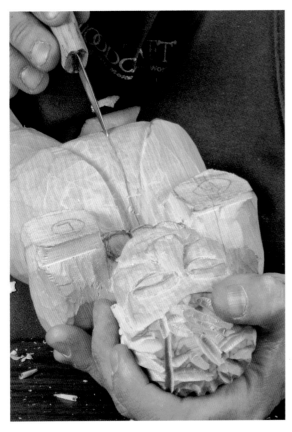

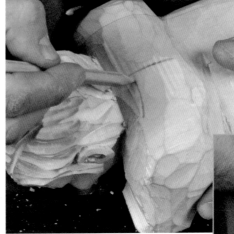

To make the collar on the coat, first draw the pattern line to represent the collar. Then use the V tool to create the edge of the collar. Trim to reshape the shoulders and arms to show the collar and to bring the arms closer to proper proportions.

Para hacer el cuello del saco, es necesario que sobre salga y se eleve por arriba de la camisa y los hombros, con una gurbia en v pequeña puede marcar el trazo y de ahí en adelante limpiar y definir el mismo con la navaja, observe la correcta proporción en los brazos y los hombros.

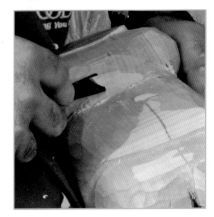

Make a little pencil line down the front of the shirt to divide it. Make the stop cut down the middle with your knife. Sharpen the knife. Use the smallest sweep to make a gouge mark on the line. This shows the front of the shirt.

Trace una línea vertical en la camisa para crear la división. Con la punta de su navaja profundice medio milímetro sobre esta línea. Con una gurbia pequeña en v remarque el corte para presentar esta división de la camisa claramente.

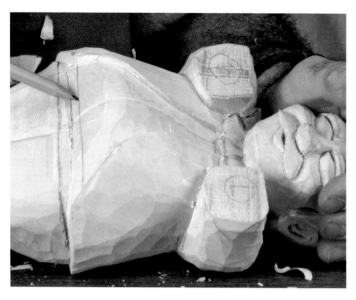 

To make the belt, draw first in the belt with a pencil. We will also draw the buckle and belt loops in time. Make stop cut above and below, along the lines of the belt. Begin to shave away excess wood from above and below the belt. The belt will now pop out.}

Para hacer el cinturón, trace con su lápiz primero y haga lo mismo que hizo en el cuello del saco, no olvide dibujar la hebilla del cinturón y las presillas del pantalón. Recuerde que las presillas es el nivel más alto en relación al cinturón.

 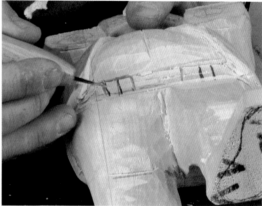

The buckle is defined with the detail knife. We have to put the belt loops in as well. The lines show you where you have to remove the wood. You are going to need to carefully remove a small amount of wood from the face to the belt to raise the loops and buckle above the surface of the belt itself.

La hebilla es tallada preferentemente con la navaja de detalle. Estas líneas muestran los límites para eliminar madera. La hebilla finalmente se muestra claramente. Recuerde las presillas las cuales sobre pasan la altura del cinturón en si.

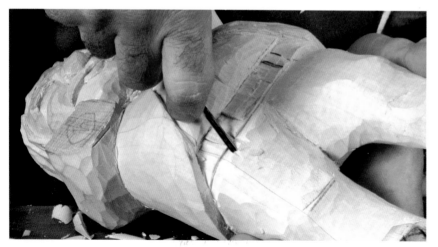

I'm adding a few small wrinkles in the pants along the belt line where the belt cinches the material with a small V gouge. Repeat this process on the shirt. You may also use a U gouge for a more natural look.

Estoy añadiendo algunas arrugas debajo del cinturón para darle una característica más real con una gurbia en v muy pequeña. Repita esto de las arrugas en la camisa y en todas las partes donde vea que la tela se dobla.

Rounding and cleaning of the leg before starting to carve the boots.

Tallando y afinando un poco más la pierna antes de tallar las botas.

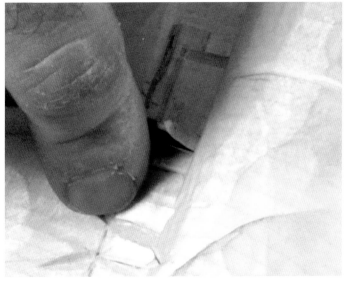

Using your detail knife, add a little detail on the buckle itself. When you are painting, the paint will really show the little details you add now. In order to make the details more prominent and clean, make sure to make deep, straight cuts on the carving to keep your carving clean and eliminate wood debris.

Con su navaja de detalle, talle en el centro de la hebilla algún detalle. Cuando ya estemos pintando la pieza, estos detalles saltan a la vista y hacen el tallado en general más interesante. Para que estos detalles resalten es necesario que salgan limpios y bien tallados. Mantenga sus cortes limpios y definidos para eliminar la micro viruta que demerita una buena talla.

Use a V tool to add a little pocket detail. Then use the detail knife to shave away some wood from below the V cut of the pocket. This will make it look deep.

Talle la bolsa lateral del pantalón. Marque con la punta de su navaja de detalle y rasure hacia la pared que marco para crear profundidad.

Using the knife to round and shape the knee.

Tallando y dándole una mejor forma a la rodilla.

Putting in the details in the mustache hair with the small V tool. Work your way up from the lower edge of the mustache to the nose. Repeat this process for the eyebrows while you're here.

Tallando los pelos del bigote con una gurbia en v pequeña. Talle de abajo del bigote hacia la nariz con mucho cuidado. Repita este proceso en las cejas ya que estamos en esto.

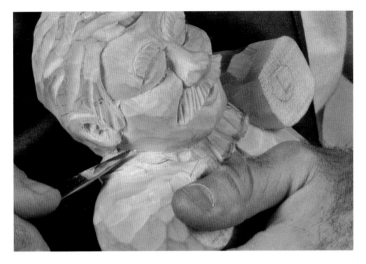

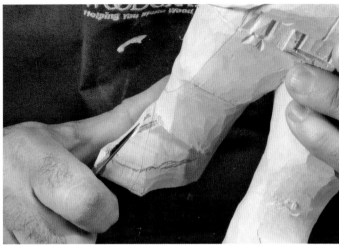

Use the bench knife to trim a little hair here at the base of the neck to neaten things up a bit.

Uso la navaja para continuar limpiando y corrigiendo detalles del cabello, el cuello etc.

It is time to begin bringing the shoes down to the proper size. Define the proper size of the shoe with a red marker crayon both on the top and bottom of the shoe. Begin to carve away the excess wood, bringing the shoe down to the marker outline shape and size.

Es momento de tallar los zapatos a su tamaño deseado. Trace la suela por debajo de los zapatos y remueva la madera tomando en cuenta los límites del trazo, lleve estos cortes a la línea exacta en el contorno de la suela. Talle despacio de abajo hacia arriba del zapato respetando los limites.

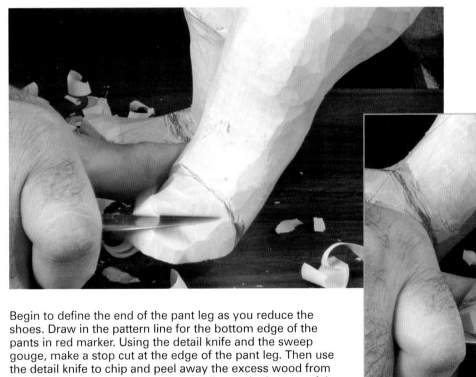

Begin to define the end of the pant leg as you reduce the shoes. Draw in the pattern line for the bottom edge of the pants in red marker. Using the detail knife and the sweep gouge, make a stop cut at the edge of the pant leg. Then use the detail knife to chip and peel away the excess wood from the shoe, working up to that stop cut line at the bottom of the pants. Start at the toe when reducing the wood, peeling back towards the pants legs at the back of the shoes. You can see how the shoe is being rounded as the excess stock is slowly removed.

Defina la parte inferior del pantalón ahora que estamos trabajando en las botas. Con la punta de la navaja defina esta vastilla del pantalón la cual empieza en el tobillo de las botas y le da la vuelta. Tomando en cuenta este trazo, márquelo con la navaja y haga un stop-cut para presentarlo claramente. Observe como el calzado se ve redondeado y tiene mas vista.

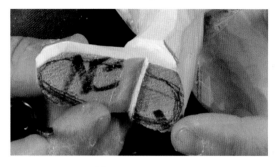

You need to carve in the details of the shoe' soles and heels. A V gouge works well for creating the line where the sole meets the upper shoe leather.

Detalle las botas, el tacón y la suela. Una gurbia en V funciona para esta tarea pero igualmente la navaja de detalle con stop-cut.

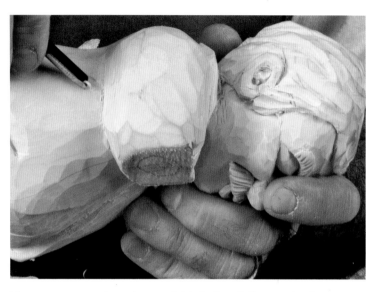
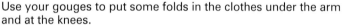
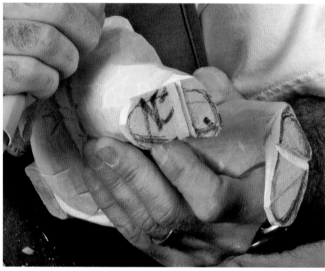

Use your gouges to put some folds in the clothes under the arm and at the knees.

Haga las arrugas con sus gurbias en U en el chaleco y los pantalones en los lugares indicados.

I like to use some fine grit sandpaper to do a general cleaning. Look over the carving to assure there are no more places to fix with a little additional carving. At some point you have to say enough is enough. For me, while I like to have the best representation, once I feel comfortable, that's enough. Sanding will sometimes take away all the square places let by the carving process, giving the piece a more finished look.

Utilizo una liga fina y doy una limpieza general a la pieza. Estudie la pieza en conjunto y asegúrese de corregir cualquier detalle a la vista con su navaja. En algún punto debemos de empezar a sentir que ya esta, punto, se acabo. Para mi cuando siento que ya esta y me siento satisfecho, pues nada, ya esta!! El lijado elimina algunas marcas no deseadas, dando una vista mas limpia.

When I am about to paint the piece, I like to cut a deep line between the garment and the skin, or between the shoes and the pants. That way the paint will run into the crack and stop there, without spreading into areas where I don't want it to go, giving a cleaner paint finish. This is a stop line for the paint. Using stop cuts in all the places where the paint will change color makes the painting so much easier.

Yo tengo la buena costumbre de separar trazando con la punta de mi navaja la separación entre todos los elementos y detalles de la pieza, de esta forma la pintura correrá hacia la grieta y se detendrá ahí sin pasarse de la línea. Es una línea límite para la pintura. Usando esta técnica en todos los lugares en donde cambiara el color hace que pintar sea mucho más sencillo.

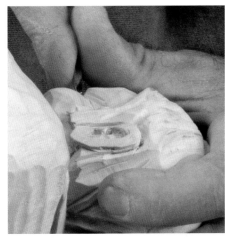

Add laugh lines to the corners of the eyes with a small V tool to add character.

Añada las líneas de expresión en las esquinas de los ojos con una gurbia pequeña en V, esto le dará más carácter al muchacho.

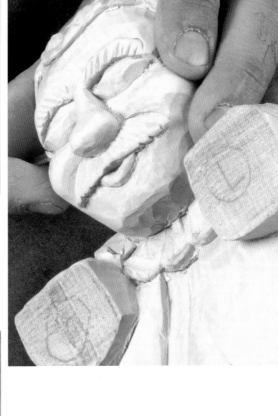

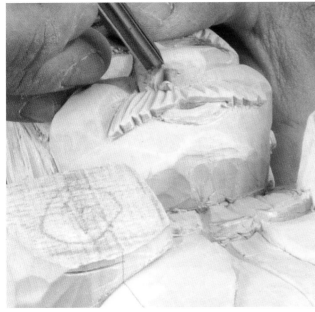

Add the nostrils with a medium sweep tool.

Añada los orificios nasales con una gurbia pequeña en U.

We are going to start on the arms now. You see the difference here? We have to make these arms fit. I compare them with the carved portions of the arms attached to the body, then carve a little off, and then compare them again. Always keep checking to ensure that you don't take off too much.

Trabajare en los brazos ahora. Observan la diferencia aquí? Tenemos que hacer que los brazos coincidan. Los posiciono en su sitio y reviso lo que debo de tallar para fundirlos con el antebrazo y que no se note el corte finalmente. Talle poco a poco con mucha atención cuidando no tallar de más.

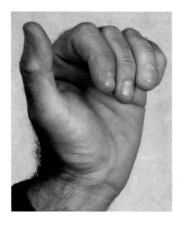 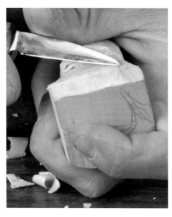 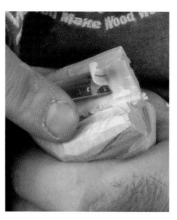 

To begin the hands, I have to look at my own hand to see how I might hold the trumpet myself. First I begin to carve the thumb. Using a red marker I draw in the pattern for the thumb and fingers. Begin trimming away excess wood. Reapply the pattern lines as you need them. We have to keep trying when carving. Sometimes you make a cut and it looks so natural and you say that is exactly the cut I was missing. Always go back to your model and make sure what you are doing is correct.

Para empezar las manos, necesito observar mis manos y analizar como tomaría una trompeta. Con un marcador, trace los dedos y el pulgar en la posición correcta. Talle estos dedos cuidando sus líneas limite, despacio vaya eliminando madera y modelando los mismos. En ocasiones cortamos con la navaja y aparece lo que buscábamos. Observe y estudie el patrón modelo de la pieza constantemente.

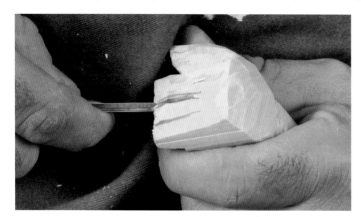 

With the V tool, make a mark for the fingers along the pattern lines. With the detail knife you make a cut between each finger. Make sure you count one, two, three, four fingers … and one thumb.

Con la gurbia en V, marque la separación entre dedos y remate con su navaja de detalle, profundizando poco a poco. Asegúrese de contar cuatro dedos y un pulgar…. Por mano.

The hand is almost right. Check the position of the hand with the roughed out trumpet.

La mano esta bastante bien. Compruebe las manos con relación a la trompeta.

  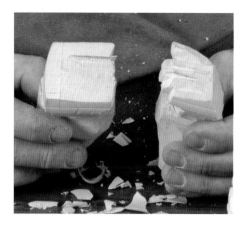

It is time to begin working on the other hand. Start by cutting the fingers. Undercut the fingers. Compare this hand with the previously carved hand and continue to remove the wood. Fit the hand to the rough trumpet, compare the hands, and see where you need to work next.

Es momento de empezar con la otra mano. Empiece por los dedos. Corte debajo de los dedos. Compare esta mano con la otra y continúe tallando. Haga que coincida esta mano con la trompeta y la otra mano, estudie bien esta situación y elimine lo que tenga que ser eliminado.

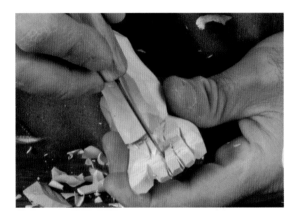 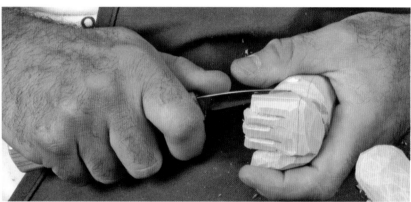

Inside the hand I cut away to reveal the fingers, following the same techniques used to cut the outside of the fingers.

Tallo por la parte interna de la mano, utilizando la misma técnica utilizada para tallar los dedos por la parte de arriba.

Carve down the arms to match, both the separated arms attached to the hands and the portions of the arms attached to the body.

Talle los brazos hacia abajo para suavizar las uniones y alinear estos con las porciones que están unidas al torso.

Here are the fingers, showing both the outsides and insides of the hands. Note how the arms have been carved as well.

Los dedos tallados, se observa el interior y exterior de la mano. Observe como los brazos han sido finalmente tallados.

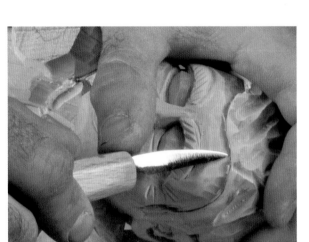

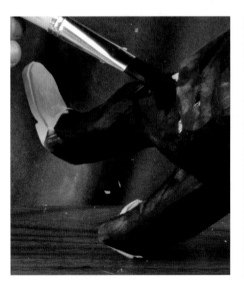

Place a stop cut under the hair a bit to give excess paint a place to go.

Separe con la punta de la navaja el cabello para que la pintura excedente se detenga en la línea.

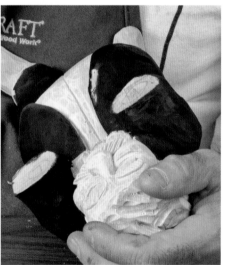

It is time to paint this Mariachi. I begin to paint by using the black acrylic craft paint. I use simple brushes. I thin the paint with water and using a large brush to begin spreading the paint evenly over the piece, use short, quick strokes that follow the grain of the wood. I always paint the darker colors first.
Continue to paint with the black until all the spots on the jacket and pants are covered. Then start a second coat. If the first coat is thin, it will dry quickly. I recommend using three coats of paint. The second coat is a little thicker than the first (less water is mixed into each brush load).

Es momento de pintar el Mariachi. Yo empiezo utilizando el color negro, la pintura que utilizo para pintar toda la pieza es acrílica. Utilizo pinceles simples. Diluyo la pintura con agua y con un pincel grueso pinto grandes áreas de una forma uniforme, siga la línea de la beta de la madera. Es conveniente pintar primero los tonos más obscuros, en este caso pinto todo lo negro. Puede ser necesario aplicar dos o más capas de pintura negra para obtener un tono fuerte y definido.

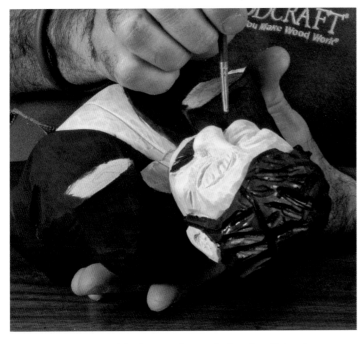

Mix brown with the black to make the hair color. Paint the mustache and the eyebrows as well.

Mezcle el marrón con el negro para dar el tono al cabello. Pinte las cejas y el bigote con el mismo tono.

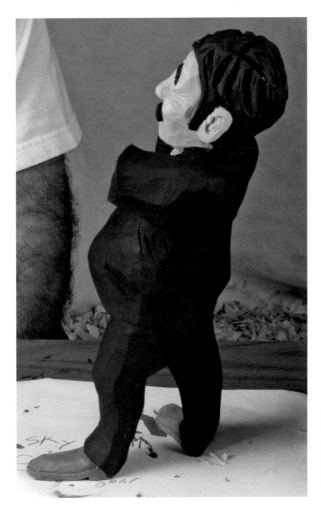

Mix white with what is left of the brown to make gray for the shoes.

Mezcle blanco con el sobrante del marrón para crear un tono gris que utilizaremos en las botas.

To make the skin color, I mix about a tablespoon of Raw Sienna with a dab of skin tone (a Jo Sonja's Decorative Paint). I mix these colors thoroughly. For a darker tone, add more Raw Sienna. For a lighter tone, add more skin tone. Put three coats of paint on the face.

Para dar el tono de piel, esta es mi receta, Mezclo aproximadamente una cucharada de Siena natural (raw Siena) con un poco de tono de piel (skin tone). Mezclo estos dos tonos. Si deseo una piel mas obscura, añado mas Siena natural y si deseo un tono de piel mas claro, añado mas tono de piel.

I forgot to put paint the belt loops black, so I'm going back to do that now. Now that the loops are finished, I need to let this guy dry for a while.

Olvide pintar estos detalles del pantalón, regreso a esto ahora. Es momento de dejar secar a este amigo un rato.

Now we are going to paint the shirt. I make a bridge with my left hand to keep my right hand steady so that I can get into the center without touching the already painted areas. If you make a mistake and get white on the black, it is really no problem, just paint over that spot with a little black.

Es momento de pintar la camisa. Con mis manos mantengo un punto de apoyo constante entre las dos para controlar el pulso y no manchar partes ya pintadas. Si mancharas un poco de blanco la zona negra no habría problema, con un poco de negro desaparece el blanco.

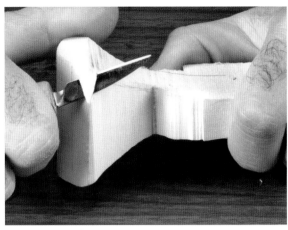

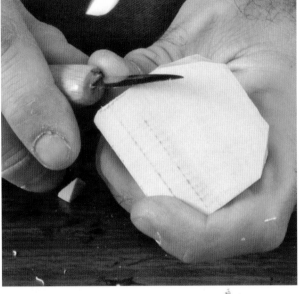

Begin rounding the trumpet with the detail knife at the flared bell end. Place some stop cuts along the trumpet's vertical lines, where the valves will be.

Empiece por redondear la parte frontal de la trompeta con la navaja de detalle. Haga estos stop-cuts en las líneas verticales, vamos, las teclas de la trompeta.

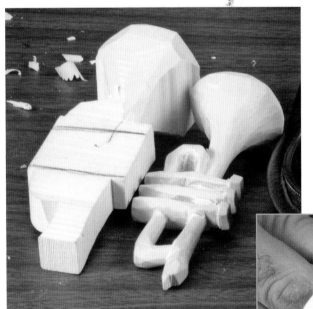

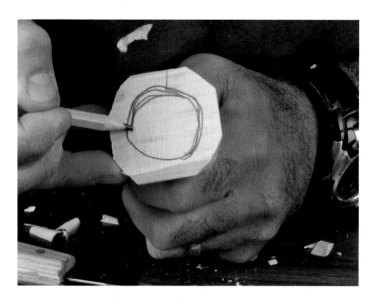
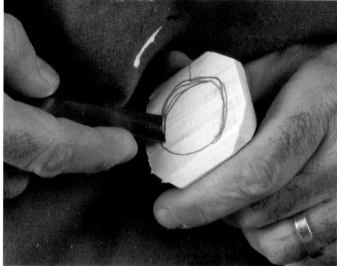

Use a pencil to outline the area of the center of the inside of the trumpet's bell. Use a sweep to dig into the center of the horn. Carving this area is working against the grain so it takes some time.

Determine y marque con lápiz el punto central del interior de la campana de la trompeta y escarbe en esa dirección hacia adentro y en forma cónica, estos son cortes en contra de la beta, tome sus precauciones y tiempo, afile sus navajas y gurbias.

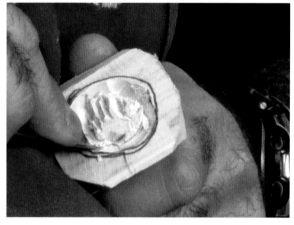
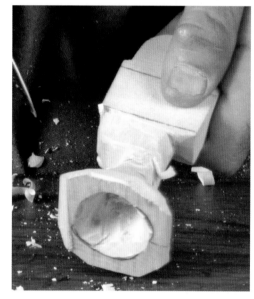

With a sweep I dug out these holes between the slides on the trumpet.

Esta gurbia me funciona para esta tarea de perforar estos canales interiores.

Round the end of the bell with the detail knife.

Redondee el borde de la orilla con la navaja de detalle.

STOP FREQUENTLY TO SHARPEN YOUR TOOLS. THIS WILL MAKE CARVING EASIER,

  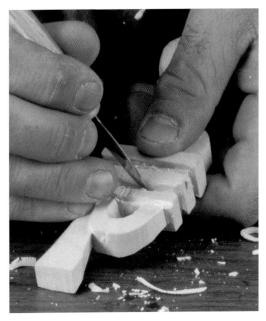

Nip away at the valve casings of the horn, rounding them a bit.

Detalle las partes de las válvulas de la trompeta redondeando un poco las mismas.

With a medium sweep mark the valve casings. Keep cutting with the sweep until you see that you can use the detail knife to get into the gouges to make them deeper.

Esta gurbia me ayuda a tallar en esta zona. Talle hasta el punto en donde requiera utilizar la navaja de detalle para acceder a esos sitios más profundos.

Continue to chip, gouge, and clean up the trumpet's form. Use the detail knife to finish the mouthpiece.

Continúe tallando y limpiando la trompeta, La navaja de detalle la uso para tallar la boquilla de la trompeta.

MORE ENJOYABLE, AND SAFER AS YOU WILL HAVE BETTER CONTROL OVER YOUR TOOLS.

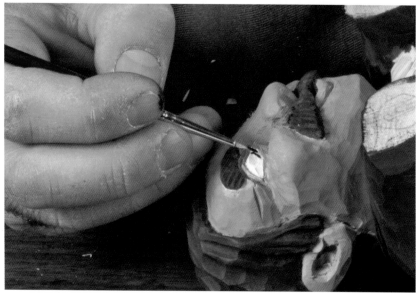

We'll pause in our work on the trumpet for now. It is time to start painting the eye. In the eye, start with white in the corner of the eyes, and then paint around what will be the iris. There are five circles in the eye. The second circle is black. The next line is medium to light brown (mixing some raw sienna into the dark brown.), which goes inside the black line.

Vamos a dejar la trompeta por el momento. Es momento de pintar el ojo. Comience por pintar de blanco las orillas del ojo, después pinte un círculo alrededor lo que será el iris.
Existen en el ojo cinco círculos. El Segundo círculo lo pinte negro. El siguiente es un café claro para que resalte, la idea es pintar círculos dentro de círculos.

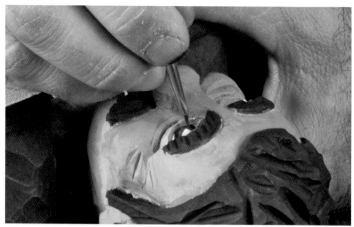

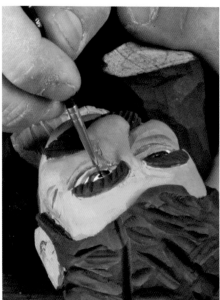

A black circle goes in the middle. Add a white dot on the pupil to show reflection and give the eyes a feeling of life.

El cuarto círculo va al centro. Añada un punto en la pupila para darle luz y vida a la mirada en los ojos.

At this point, paint the bowtie with red and allow it to dry, then apply white dots. At this time also paint the belt and buckle. Details like the buttons can be added now as well. Using a very thin wash with yellow, red, and brown, apply shadows to the edge of the face, to the sides of the nose, and under the eye, anywhere you want more shadow.

Ahora, pinte el moño con rojo intenso y deje la pintura secar, pinte puntos blancos en el moño, pinte igualmente el fajo y la hebilla. Detalles como los botones se pueden hacer en estos momentos. Usando una mezcla muy diluida y mezclada de amarillo, rojo y marrón, de sombras a todas las orillas de la cara, ojos, cejas, en fin, en donde requiera sombreado.

I use Waterproof Titebond III Ultimate Wood Glue® to glue the arms onto the figure. Allow time to dry.

Yo recomiendo el pegamento Titebond III Ultimate Wood Glue para unir los brazos a la pieza. Deje suficiente tiempo de secado.

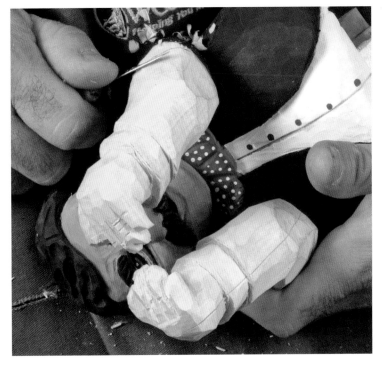
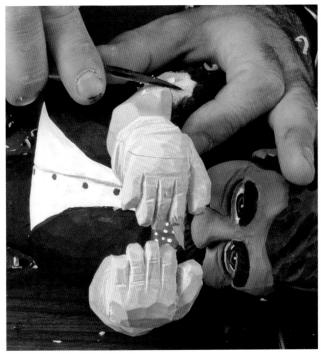

When dry, carve the arms to blend the two together, and finish shaping the arms

Ya seco, detalle las uniones para fundir ambas partes, termine el modelado de los brazos.

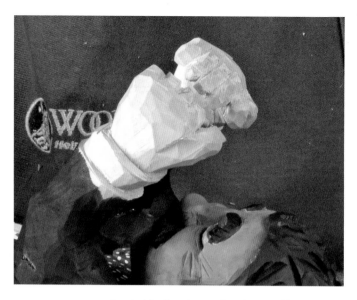

Apply black paint to the sleeves. Remember to apply three coats. Use the larger brush on most of the arm, then switch to the tiny brush for the edge of the jacket. Also use white and a small brush on the shirt cuff.

Pinte de negro las mangas. Recuerde aplicar varias manos. Utilice un pincel grande para la mayor parte del brazo y cambie a un pincel delgado y fino para delimitar las orillas. La manga que sale del saco es color blanco. Utilice un pincel pequeño.

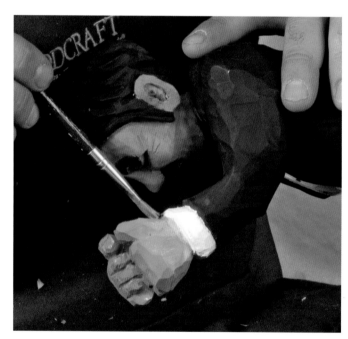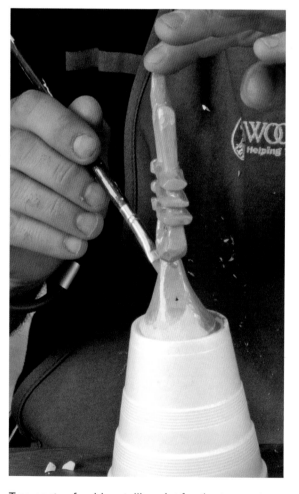

After the cuffs are painted, paint the hands. Add some shadow to the hands as well. Use a very thin wash with yellow, red, and brown to create the shadows. Put this shadow mix into all the cracks and between the fingers.

Pintadas las mangas prosiga con las manos. Añada un poco de sombras a las manos de igual forma y con la misma mezcla utilizada anteriormente (mezcla para sombrear). Rellene con esta mezcla todas las arrugas y en medio de los dedos.

Two coats of gold metallic paint for the trumpet are enough. An inverted Styrofoam cup works well as a paint stand for the trumpet.

Dos capas de pintura dorada son suficientes. Un vaso de hielo seco es efectivo para no manchar mientras seca el dorado.

Here is the rough out of the hat. It needs to be carved and painted.

Este es el bloque burdo de lo que será el sombrero charro. Necesita ser tallado y pintado.

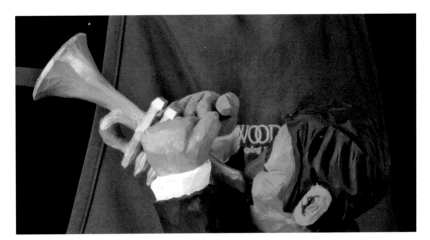

Fitting the horn into the hands to check the fit. I see that it is a good fit.

Probando que ensamble correctamente la trompeta entre las manos. Creo que están bien.

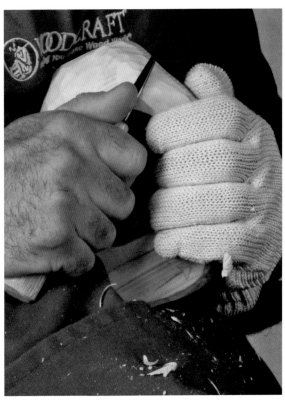

The wood of the hat has the grain going up and down from crown to brim, so it is difficult to carve. There is a lot of resistance for the knife. I use this small detail knife in this situation. When working in this close, I use this carver's mesh glove to protect my hand from a slip of the knife.

La beta del sombrero va en vertical, de la parte alta de la copa hacia el ala, por lo tanto requiere atención. Existe resistencia al corte por lo que es apropiado tallar con la navaja mas afilada, poco a poco. En ocasiones utilizo este guanto para mayor protección.

The mark on top tells me which way the hat will sit on the head.

La marca de la parte superior me recuerda el sentido correcto del sombrero.

It takes some time to carve against the grain.

Se requiere práctica para aprender a tallar en contra de la beta.

The carved hat needs a little sanding. Use fine grit sandpaper to lightly sand off the carving marks. I also need to put in some more details, such as the crease in the crown of the hat.

El sombrero requiere de un lijado fino. Utilice liga fina para limpiar y detallar la superficie del sombrero. Añado algunos detalles mas como el hundimiento de la copa superior.

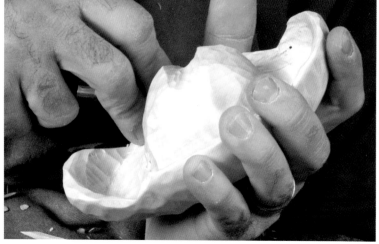

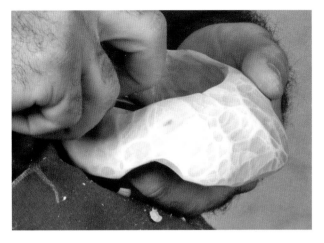

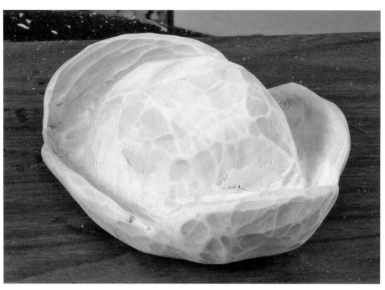

More material must come out of the hat to give it a proper fit.

Debo escarbar más para ajustar la entrada de la cabeza correctamente.

You will know when enough is enough.

Sabrás cuando suficiente es suficiente.

I think I will give this guy a small base. Cut a thin piece of wood from leftover scrap, check it against the figure to make sure it is large enough, and then soften the edge of the base with a small detail knife. Lightly sand this base and paint it. To mount the figure to the base, I use Tri-bond III Waterproof Wood Glue™. With this glue, no other fasteners are needed. Let the glue set overnight.

Voy a crear una base para este amigo. Corte un pedazo de basswood sobrante talle y suavice las orillas , sea creativo. Lije la base con una lija fina y pinte. Para montar la base al mariachi, Pegue este con pegamento para madera blanco. Con el pegamento Tribond III Waterproof Wood Glue no es necesario nada más.

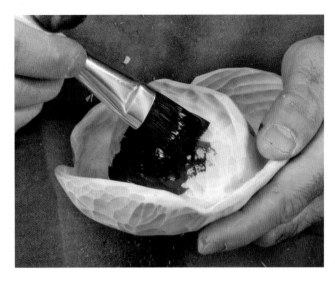

Paint the hat with several coats of black. Allow the paint time to dry.

Pinte el sombrero con varias capas de negro. Deje secar perfectamente.

With silver metallic paint, apply decorations to the Mariachi's suit. Using very tiny brushes, put small silver dots on the jacket and on the leg.

Con pintura color plata, pinte las decoraciones del traje del Mariachi. Con un pincel muy pequeño, pinte los puntos dorados en todo el traje incluyendo los pantalones.

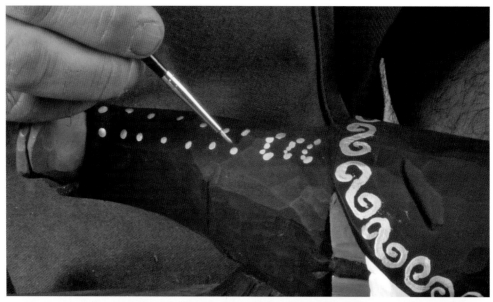

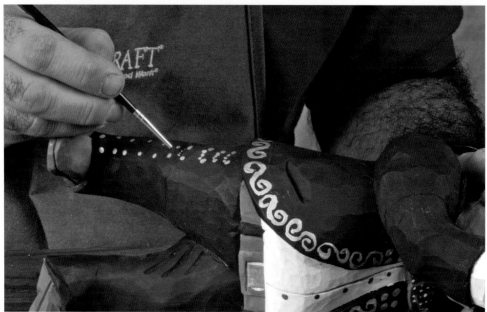

I am adding silver painted decorations on the cuffs as well. Be creative with your decoration.

Estoy añadiendo más puntos en las mangas. Sea creativo con los detalles del traje de charro.

Paint under the brim, along the edge, and on the top of the hat brim as well. Note that I am cradling my right arm in my left hand while painting, allowing me to paint within the up-curved interior brim of the hat for a steadier painting hand. This way I keep the paint where I want it. Enough is enough; it is done.

Pinte bajo la copa del sombrero y en los laterales del mismo. Con movimientos en S decore el sombrero. Una vez más apoyo una mano con la otra para tener un mejor pulso al pintar, esto me permite hacer unos trazos más simétricos.

52

Patterns Patrones

Enlarge patterns by 128 percent for a full-size pattern.

Ampliar el patrón 128 por ciento sobre estos patrones.